Usborne
First Activities

Farm Fun

Fiona Watt
Illustrated by Katie Lovell

Photographs by Howard Allman

Digital manipulation by Nick Wakeford

Fluffy lamb

1. Draw a big oval for a lamb's body.

2. Fingerpaint a black head. Then, fingerprint ears.

3. Fingerpaint four long legs. Leave the paint to dry.

4. Pull cotton balls into pieces, then roll them into balls.

5. Spread glue on the body and press on the cotton balls.

6. Glue another little cotton ball onto the head.

Muddy pigs

1. Dip your finger in pink paint and go around and around for an oval body.

2. Mix darker pink paint and fingerpaint a nose and legs.

3. Fingerpaint lots of brown mud around the pig and on its body.

4. When the paint is dry, draw a face, ears and a curly tail.

Tractor

Use a black crayon.

1. Cut a rectangle from paper. Glue it onto another piece of paper.

2. Cut out a square for the cab and glue it on top, like this.

3. Draw a big wheel at the back and a small one at the front.

4. Draw a window on the cab. Draw a funnel and some curly smoke.

5. Draw some long muddy tracks under the tractor.

6. Draw clumps of grass around the tracks.

7

Chirpy chicks

1. Draw a circle
with yellow chalk
for a chick's body
and fill it in.

2. Smudge the chalk
around and around
with your finger, to
make a fluffy shape.

Add an
eye, too.

3. Draw a beak, a
wing and legs with
an orange pencil.

4. Draw lots of little
lines around your
chick for feathers.

You could draw
lots of little
chicks together.

Printed cows

Leave the paint to dry.

1. Cut a small square of sponge. Then, pour some black paint on an old plate.

2. Dip the sponge in the paint and print squares all over a piece of white paper.

3. Cut a body and head from the printed paper. Glue them onto a piece of paper.

4. Draw four legs and two ears. Cut them out and glue them on.

5. Use a pink pencil to fill in the cow's nose. Draw two eyes and a tail.

Hens

1. Cut a half circle from a piece of patterned paper, for a hen's body.

2. Glue it onto a piece of paper, with the straight edge at the top.

3. Cut a triangle for a beak from a different piece of paper and glue it beside the body.

Draw a black dot for an eye.

4. Use bright chalks to draw legs and a wing. Add feathers on the head and tail.

You could cut
a henhouse
from patterned
paper, too.

Hay barn

1. Draw a barn and cut it out. Glue it onto a piece of paper.

2. Cut strips for the roof and cut out a window. Glue them on.

Lay the strips like this.

3. Cut two strips of sponge cloth, making one wider than the other.

4. Roll the strips together and secure them with sticky tape.

5. Spread yellow paint on an old plate. Dip the sponge into it.

6. Print lots of bales of hay inside the barn. Then, let it dry.

15

Happy horse

1. Paint a rectangle for a horse's body.

2. Paint a neck and a head. Add little ears.

3. Add four long legs beneath the body.

Draw with the
end of a brush.

4. Mix a paler shade
of brown and paint
a nose and hooves.

5. Paint a tail and
mane. Draw lines
into the wet paint.

6. When the paint
is dry, draw an eye,
nose and mouth.

17

Hairy goat

18

1. Cut thin strips of white paper, and two brown strips.

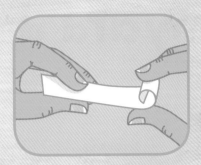

2. Roll the strips into coils, then put them aside.

3. Mix light brown paint with lots of thick white glue.

Spread the paint on thickly.

4. Paint a rectangle for a body. Add a neck, head and ear.

5. Paint four thin legs with darker hooves. Add a little tail.

6. While the paint is wet, press the white coils onto the body.

7. Unroll the ends of the brown coils. Dip one edge into glue.

8. Then, press the coils onto the head as horns, like this.

9. Paint a nose, and the inside of the ear. Draw an eye and a mouth.

Farmyard ducks

1. Draw a shape for a duck's body with a wax crayon.

2. Draw an orange beak, an eye and a little wing.

3. Fill in the body. Press firmly as you do it.

4. Draw blue lines below the body and add reeds.

5. Mix lots of watery blue paint. Brush the paint over the bottom of the duck and reeds, for a pond.

Scarecrow

1. Use crayons to draw a little hill, and a stick for the scarecrow.

2. Cut a 'T' shape from paper or fabric. Glue it on top of the stick.

3. Cut a circle for the scarecrow's head and glue it on, too.

4. Snip little pieces of string. Glue them onto the head and arms.

5. Cut out a big brown hat and glue it on top of the hair.

6. Draw a face with pencils. Glue some old buttons on his coat.

Fieldmice

Let the paint dry.

1. Draw long stems of wheat with a yellow wax crayon.

2. Dip your finger into some paint and print a mouse's body.

3. Use pencils to draw an eye, ears, a nose, feet and a tail.

Print lots of mice running up and down the stems.